FOUNDATIONS

Sixty Conversational Devotionals

by Greg W. Golden

FOREWORD

I have come to the conclusion that no one can grow and develop spiritually without a consistent and meaningful time of private devotions. That is why I am so delighted to write these words commending and introducing this resource.

Let me say a word about Greg Golden. I count this man as a dear friend and great encourager. I've known him for a number of years and have come to the conclusion that he has a personal knowledge of God. He has learned to meet with our Lord face to face and heart to heart. These devotional thoughts are not the musings of an armchair philosopher; they are gems mined from the quarry of God's Word and then polished with prayer.

I have personally read this publication, and I can attest that my own heart has been encouraged, my mind illuminated, and my will motivated to know and serve our Lord better. This material is straightforward, pertinent, free from excessive wordiness, but beautifully crafted.

I believe that you will, as I have, gain insight, be blessed, and be encouraged by Foundations. I am happy to commend them to you. I personally am grateful to God for each of the Sixty Truths given. I also believe that after a few days with this book, you will count it a treasure and then want to share another copy with a friend.

Dr. Alan Floyd
Lead Pastor
Cottage Hill Baptist Church   Mobile, Alabama

Foundations

Sixty Biblical Truths That Can Shape Your Faith

by Greg W. Golden

Scripture paraphrases are both the author's or used by permission

A Word From the Author

This book was never intended to be a book.

It began as a greeting and handshake in a small, private Christian high school gymnasium on February 7, 2024. That was where and when I met Ben. On that morning, he was being honored and presented with a scholarship to play football at a large, state university in Florida.

I had known Ben's dad for more than ten years, and I attended the signing day ceremony because God had put Ben on my heart several months earlier. I'd been praying for him, as I would my grandson or any other young man about to leave the nest and move into the college world.

Little did HE know then (and I certainly didn't know) that his life was about to experience a radical upheaval. Although tall and strong as an ox, Ben had an undiagnosed health issue that would take him away from his final semester of high school and put him in the hospital for much of the remainder of the year.

When he initially left for radiation treatments in Houston, Texas, beginning many months of procedures for cancer, I promised him to send a devotional text every day until he was able to ring the ceremonial gong following successful chemotherapy.

These 60 devotionals were the final ones of around 225 just as I wrote them and intended for my great friend Ben and him alone. However, I later shared a few of them, and then the series of sixty, with several dozen friends around the country. They encouraged me to compile them for a wider circle to read and be blessed by them, too.

So, please pull up a comfortable chair and take a seat. The pages to follow are a conversation between you and me as friends. Think of each one as a note card arriving in the mail with a fresh thought intended to uplift, challenge, and encourage you.

I'm a P.K. (a preacher's kid) and the topics here are ones that I have come to see as universally valuable to anyone who intends to grow deeper and stronger in their faith. Collectively, I think of them as foundations. Perhaps some of the insights God gave me for Ben's growth through a difficult season will resonate with you, too.

That's my prayer.

Greg W. Golden
Mobile, Alabama

For Ben

When I was 20 years old, **#1**
I surrendered my life to the
Lord. Even though I attended a
great church with an outstanding college
department, nobody told me the basics of
how to grow in my new faith. One of the
things that it took me a few years to learn
concerned the biblical requirement to be
filled with the Spirit.

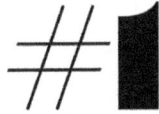

There are a few absolute commands in the
Bible, and this is one of them. It's found in
Ephesians 5:18 - *"And do not get drunk
with wine, for that is debauchery, but
be filled with the Spirit."* The sentence
structure is an imperative (present tense
verb). It means to REGULARLY and
ALWAYS be filled.

   Benefits:
   • Joy and peace in believing
   • Filled with hope
   • Empowered to be spiritually fruitful
   and make an impact
   • You'll receive guidance from God
   and understand His direction for your
   life

To be filled with the Spirit, it is

essential to:
- Daily (or even more often), ask God in prayer for this filling
- Seek to be controlled and empowered by the Holy Spirit in daily life
- Recognize and acknowledge the Spirit's presence and guidance

If you don't already do so, I encourage you to pray this simple prayer each morning, even before your feet hit the floor beside your bed. *"God, by faith, I ask you to please fill me with your Holy Spirit."* Then, expect and trust Him to do exactly that.

Should you feel your emotions and attitude slipping by noon, simply pray that again. Do it ten times a day if needed.

You might think that one "filling" in the morning would be enough. The problem with us is that *we leak!* The cares of this world and the difficulties some people bring to us mean that you and I must pay attention to our Spirit and be sure we stay filled.

The 'old man' doesn't die. #2

For the first year I walked with the Lord, my life seemed to be nearly 100 percent smooth roads and happy days. I often felt like I was going through life floating 3 feet off the ground. But, eventually, reality kicked back in, and I came down to earth.

Sinning for me during those months wasn't a big issue. Past temptations had faded dramatically. However, around the 12-month mark, I was struggling again. What was going on?!

Nobody in my church or my college pastor told me what to expect in my newfound Christian walk. I assumed that when "...*old things have passed away, and behold all things have become new*...," the old things included my old nature (called by many "the old man").

Nope! It was alive and kicking! And the old nature isn't going away until we vacate this planet and arrive in Heaven.

What happened in the new birth was that I received a NEW nature and the resources and spiritual tools to overcome and squash that "old man." But doing those things wasn't automatic! Such victories, including winning over worry, would require me to stand firm every hour of every day to be successful!

It takes intentionality, but it is entirely possible, and it is very satisfying to overcome former failures and sinful patterns.

An old saying that you have probably heard goes like this: Inside your life and mine is a black dog and a white dog. The black dog is the "old man." The white one is the new man. Someone asks you, "Which dog wins when they fight each other?" The answer for everyone is: *"Whichever dog I feed the most."*

You need an accountability partner (or two or three). #3

A TV show that was popular when I was a kid was *"The Lone Ranger."* As a former Texas law enforcer, he was a masked man who rode his horse around, preventing outlaws from harming or taking advantage of ordinary people—people who couldn't defend themselves.

But the Lone Ranger didn't ride alone. His buddy who traveled with him was a Native American named Tonto. Between the two of them, riding their horses throughout the Old West, they succeeded in their weekly missions! They also helped each other get out of tough spots because each had the other's back.

You and I need a trusted sidekick or two in life. You need a select few mature and growing Christian friends who will stick by you through the hard times and the good times. You need at least one iron-clad friend you know FOR SURE will walk IN when everyone else walks OUT.

Ecclesiastes 4:9-12 says, *"Two are better than one because they have a good return for their labor: If either of them falls down, one can help the other up. But pity anyone who falls and has no one to help them up!"* This verse highlights the value of companionship.

Key Reasons
• Shared Strengths: Two people can accomplish more together than either one can alone because they can provide support and aid to each other.
• Mutual Assistance: If one person falls or struggles, the other can lend a hand, preventing feelings of isolation or desperation.
• Toughness Under Pressure: A pair can defend themselves against foes and challenges more effectively than a lone person can. Teamwork makes the dream work!

Even beyond the obvious of one friend supporting the other, a person like this must hold the other one accountable. You need to give a select group of believing friends (those who are solid and unquestioned in their faith walk) permission to call you out if they see you heading in the wrong direction or engaging in unhealthy behaviors.

I permanently share my location using my phone 24/7 with several close brothers because I wanted to be transparent with them in our relationships. My reasoning is this: If one day they notice that I am at a bar or in a seedy part of town, they have my permission to come after me and drag me away from there. Places like that would only harm me and my testimony.

You should share your location with a few trusted friends for the same reasons and with the same permissions. I have done this thoughtfully, and they have, in the same way, given me access to their lives. You need a handful of people of strong character, and perhaps even of various ages, who you KNOW will help you by keeping you accountable and honest.

I wish I had known about the importance of "foxhole friends" and accountability partners years earlier. It would have benefited me to have positioned them around me sooner.

I should be memorizing scripture verses. #4

I will confess that Bible memorization is the most challenging thing I have ever done. How about you? I can remember the words to songs I heard on the radio dozens of years ago, but I will pull my hair out trying to memorize a simple Bible verse. I'll remember a commercial jingle word-for-word from ages ago, but I struggle to quote a scripture that points a non-believer to Christ.

Why is that?

It's because Satan knows how essential and valuable God's Word is. His demons stir up traffic jams of a thousand other thoughts in our heads when we try to memorize and meditate on the Bible.

Psalm 119:9-11 asks and then answers a question:
"How can a young man keep his way pure? By guarding it according to your Word. With my whole heart

I seek you; let me not wander from your commandments! I have placed your words in my heart so that I may not sin against God."

It's true! The way for you and me to be free from sinful patterns is to use scripture as our weapon of choice in our battle with the devil.

Hebrews 4:12 says,
"For the word of God is living and active, sharper than any two-edged sword..."
Satan cannot stand against the sword of the Word!

.

If you intend to please God with your life, follow this advice from Timothy:
"Do your best to present yourself to God as one approved, a worker who does not need to be ashamed, rightly handling the word of truth." 2 Timothy 2:15

When I memorize, I use an index card taped to my bathroom mirror. I also write the verse on a second card and wedge it onto my dashboard. I also type that verse into my NOTES phone app and then take a screenshot of it. I choose that screenshot photo as my phone's wallpaper and lock screen. That way, the verse is as close as my pocket at all times.

It has been said that the best way to memorize is to read the verse aloud seven times in the morning and seven times at night for seven days. If you do that, you will OWN that verse!

God can only remind you and me in difficult times of something we have previously learned!

Spiritual train wrecks usually happen on the heels of spiritual successes. #5

If you have a high moment of joy, a personal victory, or an answered prayer, be on notice that a slippery slope can be right around the corner, maybe even tomorrow. It's as predictable as a sunrise.

Yours and mine don't HAVE to be yo-yo lives of ups and downs like that, though, because a wise person will stay alert after a spiritual mountaintop experience.

Why is a downfall after a "high" experience so common? It occurs because while you and I are basking in the glow of some great news or following an inspiring sermon or uplifting song, Satan loves to take our eyes off our old natures and the natural tendency to sin. Pride can slip in.

This verse confirms the 5th truth:

1 Corinthians 10:12 - *"Therefore let the one who thinks he stands watch out that he does not fall."*

- Temptation is to be expected
The passage reminds us that no temptation is unique to only us; everyone faces similar tests and trials.

- It reminds us to remain humble. The verse encourages us to keep a posture of meekness (controlled strength). Realize that even those who feel strong can fall. It reminds us to examine our hearts constantly and our lives for cracks in our armor.

- The verse warns us to avoid arrogance
The verse and this 5th concept caution against the senses of self-righteousness and overconfidence. Remember that you are still mortal and always have the potential for failure.

When you experience a spiritual high time, be grateful, of course, but immediately become alerted. Your sworn enemy, the devil, loves to throw hand grenades at your feet. Again, be careful and watchful when you think you stand lest you fall!

Treading water is not an option. #6

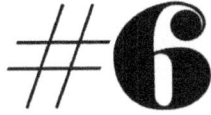

Hebrews 2:1 sets the tone for this important truth when it states, *"We must pay careful attention, therefore, to what we have heard, so that we do not DRIFT AWAY."*

The term "status quo" is Latin for "existing state"—meaning that things continuing as they currently are. That may work in some areas—such as business or relationships—but NOT in the spiritual realm.

If you have ever been swimming in a stream, a river, a gulf, or a major ocean, the water around you is in constant motion. Even a picturesque mountain brook will actively move you where it will.

I remember learning how to water ski in Kentucky on the Ohio River. We were in a protected area near the riverbank, but the current kept moving the waiting boat, me, and my skis in different directions. Not fun!

If you aren't careful and constantly correct, the locations where you enter and exit the water will be in very different places. And the exit may not be where you intended to go.

Spiritual complacency (dropping your guard) always leads to worse outcomes, never better ones. The default "pull" in our lives is distinctly downward—never up. Stay alert! No one is strong enough by themselves to withstand Satan's forces. You cannot tread water and remain in the same place. You will need to actively stand in the strength of the Lord and purposefully push back against the world's FLOW —to guard your integrity!

God's plan is better than my plan.

#7

Isaiah 55:8-9 says, *"For my thoughts are not your thoughts, neither are your ways my ways, declares the Lord. For as the heavens are higher than the earth, so are my ways higher than your ways and my thoughts than your thoughts."*

Jesus walked a fine line for thirty-three years—a path that was very narrow, very specific, and free of distractions. His Father had mapped out the road because by following it exactly, the door to eternal life for you and me would be opened.

You will remember in Matthew 4:9 when Satan tempted Jesus with an offer of Christ possessing all of the kingdoms of the world if He would simply take the exit ramp from God's plan and worship Satan (the devil's plan).

You and I can become distracted by shiny objects and alluring options.

Thankfully, Jesus remained steadfast and didn't flinch.

Maybe you would say you're unclear about God's plan for your life 5 or 10 years into the future. I would encourage you to follow this pattern:

First and foremost, don't become impatient.

• Surrender your desires. As best as you know how, you should become neutral about what you believe is best for you. God can be trusted. He wants YOUR best even more than you want it.

• If you have difficulty giving up that control, pray and ask God to help you. Ask other trustworthy people to join you in that prayer.

• Be regular in your Bible study time. God's answers will often appear in your daily reading of the scriptures.

• Enlist the counsel of wise Christians who know you well and have your best interests at heart.

• Observe the circumstances around you. Is God speaking through open doors or closed ones?

• Let the peace of God direct you. If your heart is troubled by the decision you are about to make, my best advice is to WAIT

until you have a settled spirit.
The adage is true: "When in doubt, don't!"

And until God makes the next step crystal clear, keep doing what you are doing.

"A man's heart may draw the blueprint, but the LORD determines his path." (Proverbs 16:9)

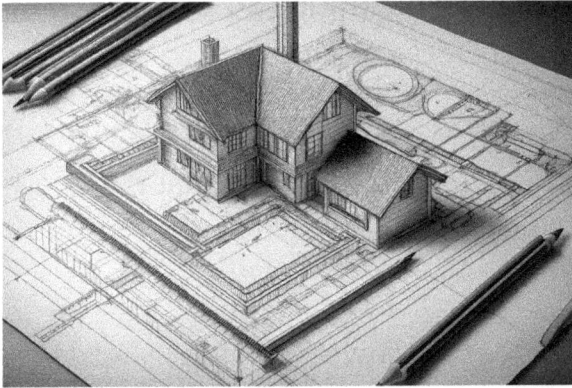

God had better NOT be your Co-Pilot. #8

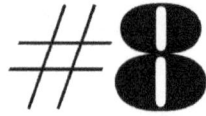

You've probably noticed license plates on the fronts of some cars stating "God Is My Co-Pilot." That claim often appears along with an image of gold or silver wings.

The slogan might seem to be clever words by a Christ-follower expressing that they and God share control of their life. The image that comes to mind is of the two of them seated side by side in the cockpit, with the Almighty maneuvering their airplane through life's challenges and storms as a team.

That's a flawed concept, erroneous theology, and it's a really bad plan!

I won't question the sincerity of the folks promoting this message, but their premise is loaded with errors.

God is absolutely sovereign. That means He is the ruler and has ALL power and authority. God will not share His throne with any human—EVER! So, to state in clever terms that you and God are going to jointly handle the controls and steer your life as a team—well, that's never been God's plan.

Jesus is Lord. Lord means 'master.' Masters don't confer with those they rule when it is time to make decisions. Rather than you or me riding up front in the left seat or even in the "shotgun" position next to God, our best choice is in the far BACK, and we should probably both go ahead and take our places in the cargo area or the trunk! God must be the commander, the pilot of your life and mine.

> *"O the depth of the riches of the wisdom and knowledge of God! How unsearchable are His judgments and untraceable His ways! Who has known the mind of the Lord? Or who has been His counselor? Who has first given to God, that God should repay him? For from Him and through Him and to Him are all things. To Him alone be the glory forever! Amen."*
> Romans 11:33-36

You need three specific people in your life! #9

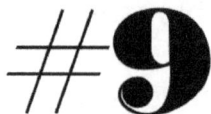

You need a Paul. A Paul is someone in your life who is mentoring you. They would be challenging you with sometimes difficult truths. This person would be uplifting you on hard days. They would be willing to answer your most challenging questions. They would establish an iron-clad connection to your life and your heart that doesn't fade or faint. They would pray for you. They would be a person who continually "calls you UP"—up to a higher and fuller commitment to Christ.

Who is your Paul?

You need a Barnabas to lock arms with and walk alongside you as you go forward. Your Barnabas might be a peer, but they should be mature in their faith. You would know them as "iron sharpening iron," making you better, and you would have the same commitment to them. A Barnabas would take a bullet for you, and you would do the same for them.

Ecclesiastes 4:9-12 helps to define what a Barnabas looks like.
"Two are better than one, because they have a good return for their labor: If either of them falls down, one can help the other up. But pity anyone who falls and has no one to help them up!"

Who is your Barnabas?

You need a Timothy. Paul had a Timothy—a younger or less experienced person to whom he committed himself—to help him grow stronger in his spiritual life.

The misunderstanding or hesitation in bringing a Timothy into your life may stem from the fact that you don't feel wise enough. If you think that, this is a good indication that with added personal discipline on your part, you can be well-suited to disciple another person. They may be younger or perhaps slightly older.

If you are a child of God, the Holy Spirit is your teacher. You have a Bible. You have life experiences that God has allowed because others need to learn what you already know about faith, hardships, and God's promises and provisions.

Having a Timothy will drive you deeper into scriptures from which to draw and teach important truths. You don't need to invent truth; instead, you must convey truths from God's word.

Who is your Timothy?

If you don't currently have a Paul, a Barnabas, or a Timothy, will you commit to be praying about and watching for each of these to be revealed in your circle?

God will forgive the sins for which I TRULY repent. #10

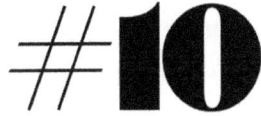

   This is a heavy truth and concept. True repentance is not the same as feeling guilty. Be clear in your understanding of how God sees our sin. Sin is an offense to God. It belittles His holiness. It is a big deal.

   True repentance includes the understanding that each sin grieves God and the Holy Spirit. Our continued sin is a statement that what Jesus did on the cross is irrelevant to me. Once this is understood, the actions that follow reveal a person's intent and heart.

   Repentance is often defined as a change of mind. That is true, but that isn't a full definition. In the context of the biblical definition, the renewed mind is also a heart change. That heart change will result in an attitude change. That attitude change will cause you to think about your life and future actions in a different way. And the outcome of this kind of change will be evident in what you do next. You will do everything possible to avoid those same sins and failures again.

The consequences of our sins do not disappear after we repent. We may have to live with them until our final breath. But after true repentance, we become *blameless* of that sin.

Having sorrow or feeling bad about what you did is not repentance. If your sin does not cause you to be grieved and changed, then you never repented, and you still bear that sin's guilt.

Always remember that ANY sin not turned away from and repented of places a barrier between us and God. He wants unbroken fellowship with you and me, but being holy, He cannot excuse us, hear our prayers, and extend blessings to us if we willingly harbor sin.

The best part of this subject is what we learn from Hebrews 8:12 when we fully repent. God says, *"I will forgive their sins and no longer remember their wrongs."*

God's plan to reach the world with the good news of the gospel has always included us.

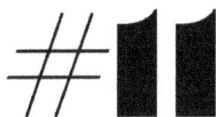

#11

There is a widely shared tale that takes you and me back to the year 33 A.D. when Jesus ascended into Heaven.

According to the story, the angel Gabriel met Jesus upon the Savior's arrival in Paradise. Gabriel cringed when he saw the scars from the crown of thorns and the marks from the cruel spikes that tore through Jesus' wrists and feet.

Gabriel said, "Master, you suffered terribly for those down on earth."

"Yes, I did," Jesus replied.

Gabriel continued, "Do they all know about your great sacrifice and understand your offer of forgiveness and eternal life?"

"No, not yet," said Jesus. "Right now, only a limited number of people in my home country know about my death and resurrection and my desire for all to receive forgiveness and spend eternity in Heaven."

Gabriel looked perplexed, and the angel asked, "Then, how will everyone learn about these wonderful things?"

Jesus responded, "Before I left, I instructed Peter, James, John, and a handful of friends and followers to tell all people and nations about them. And when those new converts hear and believe, they, in turn, will tell more people. And I intend that the whole earth will eventually hear about the gospel story."

Troubled, the angel responded, "But what if your followers become weary or lazy? Or what if they DO tell the story, but the next generation becomes distracted with other pursuits? What if centuries from now, people aren't committed any longer to your great commission? Have you made other plans?"

The Lamb of God looked into the face of the angel Gabriel and said, "I have no other plan. I am counting on those whom I have redeemed."

You have a testimony of God's grace and goodness, and so do I. You have a voice, and so do I. You owe a debt to the Lord Jesus, and so do I. We are both parts of His plan. We cannot fail Him.

You have at least # 12 one spiritual gift given to you when you were born again. Learn about it and pray for opportunities to use it.

There are Gifts of the Spirit (also known as the Fruit of the Spirit). They are love, joy, peace, gentleness, patience, etc. What I'm talking about here is different from those.

God is pleased when you practice your spiritual gift—the unique one He has given you. In fact, He has designed the church to work best when everyone exercises their gifts.

When you were saved, God equipped you with a PRIMARY spiritual gift and likely a couple of secondary gifts. See if you recognize your primary gift. Then look for your secondary gift(s), as well.

1. **Prophecy** - They speak the word of God to others to expose sin and restore relationships
2. **Serving** - They are driven to demonstrate love by meeting practical needs
3. **Teaching** - They are passionate about discovering and validating truth from the Bible
4. **Exhorting** - They want to see believers grow to spiritual maturity
5. **Giving** - This person wants to use finances wisely to be able to give to meet the needs of others
6. **Organizing** - They can solve problems and accomplish tasks by evaluating problems and designating others to help.
7. **Mercy** - He or she is sensitive to the emotional and spiritual needs of others and wants to help them.

You and I never want to become prideful about our gift. It is nothing we can take credit for. God gives it (and can take it away) at His discretion.

It is essential that you identify yours and then utilize it! The church body needs your giftedness to function fully!

If you can cut it and it bleeds, it's not your enemy! #13

Spiritual warfare is real, but God and Satan aren't nearly in the same league.

The Bible tells us that the number of created angels is "innumerable" and "countless." We know the prophet Daniel saw 100 million angels in Heaven kneeling before God's throne. Those are only a portion of the number of angelic beings assigned to minister to those on earth who are being drawn toward salvation and those who are children of God.

Before people inhabited the earth, one-third of the created angels were deceived by Satan and fell from Heaven with him when he was cast out. Those are the demons who attack and oppress humanity. Again, we have no idea what that total number is, but it is vast!

Ephesians 6:12 says: *"For we wrestle not against flesh and blood, but against principalities, against powers, against the rulers of the darkness of this world, against spiritual wickedness in high places."*

If our eyes could be opened to the battles that take place in the spiritual world—battles the demons are constantly waging around you and me to place temptations and evil thoughts into our minds, we would be terrified. But as a Christian, you have even MORE angels fighting to guard and protect you from Satan's forces.

"This Present Darkness" written by Frank Peretti paints a vivid picture in a fictional setting of the extent of satanic activity in the world today. There are two dangers in considering spiritual warfare: overplaying the devil's influences around us and minimizing his activity. He would very much like for us to do the latter.

Sometimes, I shake my head in wonder at the extent of evil in today's world and how many seemingly normal people are promoting it. It's nothing new because Satan has been trying to embarrass Jesus and undercut God's work since before Adam and Eve. And the Bible tells us it will only worsen as the end times come.

Be alert and wear your spiritual armor using the word of God (the Bible) as your sword of offense and defense.

"Greater is He who is in me than he who is in the world!" 1 John 4:4

I need to understand the difference between feeling guilty and experiencing conviction. #14

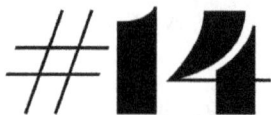

When the unsaved person sins, they may experience a pang of guilt for their actions. That feeling may lead them to "turn over a new leaf" or resolve to "do better" next time (i.e., making New Year's Resolutions). Those responses are helpful, but are external and driven by the desire to feel better about yourself. They don't bring about a change of attitude at the heart level.

What is usually lacking in man's sense of guilt is true repentance.

When a follower of Christ sins, the Holy Spirit, who resides in each Christian, initiates an understanding that their sin is grievous to God, that their actions have broken their fellowship with Him.

Satan's counterfeit counterpart to godly sorrow is GUILT. Guilt is the devil's effort to make a Christian feel worthless—that he has gone too far with his sin, that the rift created is too deep.

God doesn't do that. God's desire at all times is for restoration.

The parable of the prodigal son is the biblical example of God's wish and plan to bring the wandering son or daughter back into fellowship.

Satan loves to crush us with guilt. If you feel guilt that offers you condemnation with no hope for a return to fellowship, that is Satan talking. God will reveal your sin through the Holy Spirit's conviction, lead you away from your failures, and then shine His light on the pathway back (repentance) to restoration and full fellowship with Him.

Learn to discern the differences between Satan's debilitating guilt and God's restoration through sorrow and repentance.

You are tallest when you're on your knees.

#15

That seeming contradiction is called a paradox, and the Bible contains many of them. In this paradox, your humble prayer position transports you immediately into the throne room of Heaven.

Other paradoxes from the scriptures are:
• We see unseen things. (2 Corinthians 4:8)
• We find life by losing our life (Matt. 10:39)
• When we are weak, we are made strong (2 Cor. 12:9-10)
• When we humble ourselves, we are lifted up (James 4:10)
• We conquer by submitting. (Romans 8)
• We become great as we serve. (Mark 10)
• We are made first when we choose last. (Matthew 20:16)
• We receive when we give. (Luke 6)
• We find victory in infirmities. (2 Cor. 12)
• We find rest under a yoke. (Matthew 11:29)
• We become free by being bondservants. (1 Cor. 7)

The wisdom of the Word of God will always confound those who are not following Christ.

You have exactly the correct number of available minutes in your day to fulfill God's plans for you.

#16

If you run out of minutes and hours before completing your tasks for the day, you've strayed from the best things along the way.

That may sound harsh. Indeed, unforeseen circumstances can arise; however, this axiom is generally provably true.

If you are too busy to spend time with the Lord, you're just too busy. You are out of balance. God won't wait in your queue and accept the reasoning of *"…if I finish with this or that, then I'll give Him leftover moments for some hurried Bible reading and a quick prayer."*

2 Timothy 2:15 says Make it a priority to... *"study to show thyself approved unto God, a workman who needs not be ashamed, rightly dividing the word of truth."*

If you have more things on your plate than the hours to handle them, don't hesitate to evaluate. Always give God the first fruits of your time.

God can do more with 90% than I can with 100%. #17

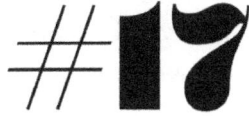

What do you see as the typical reaction of a person when they hear that the morning's sermon will be about tithing?
I'll bet it is one of these:
- Tune it out
- Become antsy or irritated
- Become defensive
- Or nod in agreement over the privilege of giving to the Lord from your resources

Growing up in a one-income and barely middle-class family, I watched my parents tithe as they depended on the Lord for our needs. My dad served on the staff of small churches, oftentimes volunteering his time. Later, he was a school teacher in the days when they were underpaid. Faithful to God's words and promises, He *"supplied all of our needs according to His riches in glory!"*

The promise to bless the tithe is found in Malachi 3:10 - saying, *"Bring the full tithe into the storehouse, so that there may be food in my house, and thus put me to the test, says the Lord of hosts."* The verse continues, *"See if I will not open the windows of heaven for you and pour down for you an overflowing blessing."*

My parents explained to us that many of the promised "blessings" weren't financial but instead included ongoing physical health among our family members. We had no serious sicknesses, and we loved each other. We experienced no major stresses or strife.

When I hear people moan and complain about a tithing sermon, I know immediately where their hearts and treasures are centered.

But tithing isn't only about money. It refers equally to our time and talents. Volunteering to teach 4th-grade boys in a Life Group is a form of tithing your time. Coaching a group of inner-city kids in the sport you love is a method of tithing your talents.

I hope you saw this demonstrated in your home. It's not something you wait to begin until you are married with kids and a mortgage. I learned by example to tithe my finances, starting with my after-school job at a grocery store when I turned 16.

God doesn't need your money or mine. But He wants us to acknowledge who and what we depend on as our source. He wants our trust to be in HIM, not ourselves or our resources. Tithing demonstrates that we are trusting God for everything.

The fact is, it's ALL His anyway. He allows those who tithe to keep 90%—which supernaturally exceeds the full 100%.

Either I judge my sins, or God will judge them. #18

This one is another heavy topic, so let's drill down on it together.

We know what the ultimate duty of a judge is. It's to be sure that the sentence for a particular crime is administered (carried out). We also know that because of the fall of Adam and Eve, God, as judge, pronounced, *"The soul that sins, it shall die."* (Ezekiel 18:20)

That sounds harsh—to experience death because of sin. We understand that this sentence of death never refers to PHYSICAL death. No person alive or who has ever lived will cease to exist because the "person" isn't the body. The "person" is the spirit—their soul. Our bodies may go into the grave, but our spirits and those of others will enter eternity the very second our heart stops beating.

We have the opportunity at any point in every day to come clean concerning our sins and pronounce a sentence over them. If we do this, God won't need to.

Repenting of my sin requires putting my "old man"—the old nature—to death by identifying with Jesus's death because Jesus died FOR MY SIN.

2 Corinthians 5:14 says: *"One died for all, therefore all died."*

That concept has always been difficult for me to comprehend fully. The best explanation I've heard is this: God put the sins of all humankind into Adam and declared us all sinners by nature and choice. It also happened that on the cross, He (God) put the sins of the whole human race INTO Christ Jesus (called "the Second Adam") so He could bear those sins and pay for them with His death. When His Father raised Jesus from the grave, He declared those people righteous who, by faith, accepted that payment for themselves.

If we declare that our sinful actions are grievous to God and agree with Him that Jesus needed to die to cleanse us, then we have executed judgment over that sin.

We must do this every time the Holy Spirit reveals our sins to us.

If we DON'T declare our sinful actions as grievous to God, then God must execute judgment over that sin (and over us). Fellowship with God will be broken until we acknowledge and repent of our sins. But that fellowship is restored instantly once we judge ourselves!

Either we acknowledge and leave our sins, or God will have to deal with us over them.

Gathering for corporate worship **#19**
is not an option that I can take or leave. The collective church is Jesus's idea.

I grew up in the church from my nursery years through high school. You might make the same claim. My family attended on Sunday mornings, evenings, AND Wednesday nights. It was the tradition of my parents.

During my first two years of college, I consciously chose to take a break from attending church. Without going into the details, my actions have caused me regret, which I still carry today. I lost opportunities for influence with close friends—people I care deeply about—many who are still without Christ.

The apostle Paul said: *"Let us not neglect the assembling of ourselves together (church meetings), as some people do, but encourage and warn each other, especially now that the day of his coming back again is drawing near."* (Hebrews 10:25)

And why is that?

God places great importance on us as the Bride of Christ—the church—as redeemed people, fellowshipping and worshipping together. He knows our tendencies to move apart and not closer together. You and I cannot grow in our Christian faith by being a "stand-alone" Christian. We all need each other, and God designed us for close relationships with those who share our faith.

The building isn't the church. The believers are. You can be 100% obedient and in fellowship with the Lord by attending a home group or a house church. Much of the world worships this way out of necessity. Those are fine, but this approach is a supplement to the joining of our voices and locking arms with multiple others who bring different life experiences into our world. You and I need the accountability of other believers in regular and up-close fellowship.

If you've ever tended a fireplace or a charcoal grill, you understand that an ember grouped next to other embers will glow warm and bright. But if you pull that ember away from the concentration of the other embers in the fireplace, the lone one will grow dark and quickly begin to cool. An individual church member draws much of their effectiveness from the entire "fire." When alone we fade quickly.

I wish I had heeded that scripture from Hebrews sooner. I would have spared myself two wasted years.

Please learn from my mistake and make church attendance one of your non-negotiables today and twenty years from today!

You can have #20
as much
of Jesus
as you want.
You have as much of Jesus
as you want.

Those sentences aren't typos or mistakes. Read them again.

The words above might be affirming to you because your heart and life may already be full and overflowing with God's presence and peace. Only you and God know.

Those words might be convicting to you because you see the need to spend more time with your Bible open, in prayer, and leading others to faith in Christ. Only you and God know.

Whichever is true for you, God is beyond our understanding. We can never fully comprehend Him or exhaust Him.

But He invites us to an intimate relationship with Himself.

If you see that there is room for MORE of Jesus' power and peace in your life, consider James 4:8. Simply...

"Draw near to God, and
He will draw near to you."

Notice the two parts of this verse. First is your part, followed by God's part. We initiate, and then He responds. It's a promise!

The higher the berries grow on the bush, the sweeter the flavor!

#21

I am not a Horticulturist or an Orchardist, nor do I know anyone who is. However, I have picked many varieties of fruit from trees. In my experience, the sweetness comes from the satisfaction of gleaning from the higher branches of the trees and bushes after other shorter people (I am a tad over six feet tall) have come, made their selections, and gone. The good stuff is harder to acquire, but I maintain it tastes better.

Be forewarned that following Christ—*really* pursuing a holy life—is hard, it's costly, and it will stretch you. Jesus must become your PRIORITY. Speaking to a large crowd, Jesus said, "*If anyone comes to me and does not hate his father and mother, his wife and children, his brothers and sisters—yes, even his own life—he cannot be my disciple. And anyone who does not carry his cross and follow me cannot be my disciple."* (Luke 14:26-27)

Jesus emphasizes counting the cost, using analogies like building a tower or a king going to war, underscoring that discipleship requires total commitment, PRIORITIZING Him above family, possessions, and even one's own life. Jesus must take precedence over all relationships, possessions, and personal ambitions.

SELF-DENIAL will take center stage for a true disciple. It will become apparent as you surrender your personal desires and comfort to God's will.

Mark records in his writings quoting Jesus: *"Whoever wants to be my disciple must deny themselves and take up their cross and follow Me."* (Mark 8:34)

Jesus, in Luke 9:23 is quoted adding the word "daily," and stressing that following Him involves sacrifice and a shift in what you deem essential. He warns that gaining the world but losing one's soul is futile. Jesus emphasized that it is an ongoing and lifelong commitment

There must come a SACRIFICE, a willingness to bear a "cross" that symbolizes suffering, persecution, or even death.

As hard as these are to undertake, the benefits—the sweetness of it all—make it worth every sacrifice and effort.

God will fight my battles for me. I only need to take a seat, trust Him, and watch. # #22

One of my favorite Old Testament stories comes from a time when Moses was leading the Israelites through enemy territory. They encountered the Amalekites, and Moses instructed his spokesman, Joshua, to select capable men from the Israelites and engage them in battle. Moses said that he would go to the top of a mountain and observe the battle from there.

So Moses took his rod and two trusted friends, Aaron and Hur, and together they ascended to a high vantage point to observe the two groups of opposing warriors.

During the battle below them, as long as Moses held his arms up, the Israelites would win. But when Moses became tired and lowered his hands, the Amalekites began to gain the upper hand.

His friends told him to sit on a rock, and from that position, they held up Moses' hands. When they did that, Israel prevailed.
At the end of the day, Israel won the battle.

God will fight for you. Just release your concerns to Him and raise your hands in trust and worship. Even when you tire, He will "make a way" for you and reward your praise.

Sometimes, that "way" involves caring friends.

Our hope isn't now and never has been in the world system and earthly things. #23

Don't look to this world or your abilities to achieve your dreams because...
"My God shall supply ALL of your needs according to His riches in glory."
Philippians 4:19

Psalm 33:20-22 tells us,
"We put our hope in the Lord.
He is our help and our shield.
In Him, our hearts rejoice,
for we trust in his holy name.
Let your unfailing love surround us, Lord,
for our hope is in you ALONE."

1 John 2:15-17 says, *"Don't love this evil world and all that is in it, for when you love the world's things, you show that you do not truly love God; for all these worldly things, these evil desires—the craze for sex, the ambition to buy everything that*

appeals to you, and the pride that comes from wealth and importance—these are not from God. They are from this evil world itself. And this world is fading away, and these evil, forbidden things will go with it, but whoever keeps doing the will of God will LIVE."

My role in the #24 Kingdom is simply to tell the Good News. God's role is to draw people to Himself. Understanding this, I am hereby released from the burden to 'save' anyone.

For much of my Christian life, I felt obligated to get as many people as possible on their knees and for them to pray the sinner's prayer. That pressure came from well-meaning people but never from the Bible or God.

There must first be the Holy Spirit drawing someone to open their eyes and reveal a person's need for forgiveness of their sins. I can't do that, and was never asked to.

God has a timetable for everyone

everywhere to hear from Him at least once concerning their spiritual poverty. This includes people in primitive settings often found in the darkest corners of the globe. I am not privy to His timing or plans.

So my job and your job is to stay "locked and loaded" and ready to share the gospel—and how it changed us.

2 Timothy 4 is our mandate.
"Tell the good news of God urgently at all times, whenever you get the chance, in season and out, when it is convenient and when it is not."

My responsibility to share the good news of the gospel extends as far and wide as my circle of influence.

#25

Acts 1:8 tells us:
"You will receive power when the Holy Spirit comes on you, and you will be my witnesses in Jerusalem, and in all Judea and Samaria, and to the ends of the earth."

Research has shown that the average person is connected to and known by 600 people. You have a degree of influence with them—some, obviously, more than others. So, that group represents your "Jerusalem"— your inner circle.

When the opportunity comes to speak your witness to one of those 600, you'll recognize it by a tug in your heart and butterflies in your stomach. It's the classic sign that God has brought them and you together and has paved the way for a spiritual encounter.

Remember from my last message that it's not your responsibility to "save" anyone—only to TELL—to tell them the good news of what happened to you.

You are not responsible for MY circle of friends. They won't listen to you. And I am not responsible for sharing the gospel message with your 600. They don't know me and aren't interested in what I have to say.

If the joy of the Lord is real and present in your life, pray for opportunities to share with whoever will listen what has changed you. That's a prayer God loves to answer.

If I am half-hearted toward God I am completely useless to God.

#26

A half-hearted person has one foot in the world and one foot pursuing righteousness, but they are a complete failure in spiritual matters.

Half-heartedness leads to spiritual stagnation. Such a person is unable to enjoy God's promises.

Examples are:
2 Chronicles 25:2 reminds us that *"King Amaziah did what was right in the eyes of the Lord, yet not with a whole heart."* God punished his kingdom for the king's attitude and decisions.

A half-hearted person is corrupt and wishy-washy. James 4:8: *"Purify your hearts, you double-minded."*

Psalm 86:11: *"Unite my heart to fear your name."*
David prayed this because he recognized his error and felt deep regret.

Hosea 10:1-2: *"Your heart is divided; Now you are held guilty."*
The prophet Hosea warned the nation about what would happen when the heart is divided.

These verses emphasize the importance of having a unified heart focused on God rather than being divided between worldly and spiritual desires. A divided heart will lead to instability, guilt, and a lack of spiritual depth.

A single-minded heart also comes from choices we each make regarding our non-negotiables— those "red lines" we must never compromise on or cross.

Real love confronts.

#27

Recently, I sat in the living room of a friend. This fellow is a wonderful person, newly married, and highly intelligent. Two other close acquaintances and I arrived at his front door that night without any advance notice.

The three of us love him. Any of us would take a bullet for this person if that situation ever arose.

We went there because our friend's life had veered into a ditch. He knew it, and we knew it. He had left the "door" to his life ajar, and the devil eased in with a foothold that became a stronghold and eventually took over as a stranglehold.

For the longest time, our friend thought he had hidden his dark habit from everyone and was able to manage it. What began as something seemingly innocent became devastating and life-altering.

It always ends that way when we listen to our appetites and buy into the world system. It's just like tiny termites undermining a house that appears strong and solid, but behind the walls, the structure is crumbling and worthless.

The 90 minutes at his home were awkward for all of us. But REAL LOVE confronts. Fake love tolerates.

Our example to follow is found in the Old Testament, in 2 Samuel chapter 4. King David had committed adultery with Bathsheba. His sin caused a pregnancy. In his attempt to conceal his actions, he arranged for the death of Bathsheba's husband.

Two grievous sins had taken place. You know this story. David thought he had masterfully hidden his sin from everyone, but God revealed it to his friend Nathan. God sent Nathan with the high-risk task of confronting David.

Nathan's intervention took place in the grand palace. Ours happened in a suburban home.

David, as King, had the royal authority AND his guards in the next room, so if he had merely flicked his little finger, that gesture would have resulted in Nathan's swift death.

But God was with Nathan. And David repented when he was lovingly confronted.

A quote attributed to David Jeremiah says: "*Sin takes you farther than you planned to go. It keeps you longer than you planned to stay. And it costs more than you expected to pay.*"

The warning to my friend and us all is to run from what you know to be your weakness. Guard your heart, avert your eyes, and purify your body and thoughts. Close, lock, and seal that "door!"

The only things you can take to Heaven with you are people. #28

John D. Rockefeller was the wealthiest man alive during the early 20th century. His net worth in the 1930s was nearly a billion dollars. In today's economy, that amount would be a staggering figure!

Rockefeller was often heard to say that the money he possessed was never enough. He made most of his fortune in the oil industry. He was a ruthless and hated man.

When he died in 1937 at the age of 97, everyone asked the question, "How much money did he leave?" The simple answer was, "He left it all."

Jesus told a story in Luke 16 of a rich man who had a large harvest. *"He thought to himself, 'What shall I do? I have no place to store my crops.' Then he said, 'This is what I'll do. I will tear down my barns, build bigger ones, and store my surplus grain there. And I'll say to myself, "You have plenty of grain laid up for many years. Take life easy; eat, drink, and be merry." But God said to him, 'You fool! This very night, your life will be demanded of you. Then who will get what you have prepared for yourself?' "This is how it will be with whoever stores up things for themselves but is not rich toward God."*   Luke 12:16-21

We cannot take our possessions with us to Heaven, but the one thing we CAN take is an unlimited number of people, through our faithful words and loving witness to others.

Acts 13:47 *For this is what the Lord has commanded us: "I have made you a light for the Gentiles, that you may bring salvation to the ends of the earth."*

Be careful not to become self-satisfied and smug because of the sinful and destructive things you DON'T do.

#29

This list applies to those who closely follow Christ as disciples. We don't smoke, drink, cuss, or chew. We don't do drugs, and we don't gamble. We don't engage in illicit sex. These are all physically or emotionally destructive, and they are all sins of COMMISSION—sins people commit.

As important as it is to abstain from those destructive practices, this is only half-obedience, according to James 4:17.

What does that mean?

Knowing what is WRONG to do and not doing it is ADMIRABLE. But, the verse in James says, *"Knowing what is RIGHT to do and NOT doing it is A SIN."*

It is a sin to withhold good when it is within my power to do good. If someone comes to you with a legitimate need, and you turn them away while having the means to assist, that becomes a sin of OMISSION for you. You failed to help when you could have. Other examples are
• Not praying
• Not standing up for what is right
• Not sharing Christ with others
• Not being encouraging when we could be
• Disregarding the urging of the Holy Spirit

Although these examples of INACTIONS are not always spelled out in the Bible, the Holy Spirit, through your conscience, will always help you discern between these two categories. Be careful to be obedient.

Once again, *"Knowing what is right to do and not doing it is a sin."* James 4:17

'Love ya!' is not nearly the same as 'I love you!' Jesus didn't say 'Love ya,' and neither will I. #30

From cover to cover, the Bible is full of examples of God's unfathomable love for us. In those pages, we read of these common types of love:

• God's and Jesus' Agape Love: Wanting the highest good for someone else. This is unconditional, selfless, and sacrificial love, demonstrated by God's actions toward us and Jesus' love. He showed us by His teachings, miracles, and His sacrifice on the cross

• Brotherly love: The love and care shown among believers, as seen in the relationships between Jesus' disciples, including Peter and John, and between Paul and Timothy

• Family love: Like the love Boaz had for Ruth or Abraham for Isaac

• Friendship/Philia love: The deep and committed friendship between David and

Jonathan, and the affection between Paul and his fellow apostles

The New Testament, which is only a partial record of Jesus' ministry on earth, has no less than nine recorded statements of Jesus saying "I love you!" to different people or groups of people.

In the upper room, Jesus didn't tell his disciple John, "Luv u buddy."

The good Samaritan didn't merely "luv" the wounded man.

Jesus said that he loved—not "luv'd"—Martha and Mary.

None of these examples are half-hearted or casual expressions of Jesus's love for those around Him.

Jesus spoke instructions to you and me in the Upper Room as He spent the final and crucial hours with His disciples. John 13:34 records this: *"A new command I give you: Love one another. As I have loved you, so you must love one another."*

Why do so many people resist that expression and seem unwilling to tell friends and family of their love? Maybe they haven't heard those words often from others, if ever. Those three words seem to stick in their throat.

Maybe they equate that word with "eros" love—sexual attraction. That is not how Jesus modeled love for us—and even instructed us to express it.

Once again, Jesus didn't say "Luv ya'" to His disciples and friends—and neither will I!

Our unrepented "secret sin" on earth is an open scandal in the throne room of Heaven.

#31

Luke 12:3 tells us an unwelcome truth. *"What you have said in the dark will be heard in the daylight, and what you have whispered in the ear in the inner rooms will be proclaimed from the roofs."*
Luke 8:17 goes a step further when it says,. *"For all that is thought to be secret will one day be brought into the open, and everything that has been hidden will be brought into that light and made known to all."*

The principle you and I must understand is that God knows, sees, and hears the actions we commit, and He is equally aware of the intentions that emanate from our hearts. Romans 14:12 warns us that each person is responsible to God for their acts AND thoughts.

Wait a minute! Our thoughts, too? Proverbs 23:7 states that our thoughts are the incubator of our actions; therefore, we will be held accountable for unbridled thoughts.

I've heard it said that my character—the *REAL* me—is who I am when I'm alone in a room with the door closed, the windows locked, and the shades drawn. Because during the times when people are watching, I can wear a mask to cause friends, family, and the public to see and think what I want everyone to believe—everyone but God. He isn't fooled. He knows the deep recesses and intentions of your heart and my heart.

Why not make this your motto: *"The Lord detests lying lips, but he delights in people who are trustworthy."* (Proverbs 12:22)

God doesn't just ALLOW troubles, He also SENDS troubles. #32

He does this so we won't depend on ourselves. But, with the troubles, He provides the precise amount of strength to sustain us.

Proof:
In 2 Corinthians 12:7, Paul tells us that God sent a *"thorn in the flesh"* so he would not become prideful. Paul said that in this hardship, he was glad to be a *"living demonstration of God's power."*

But, in our difficulties: *"God is our refuge and strength, always ready to help in times of trouble."*
Psalm 46:1

"He meets the needy in their trouble and gently bears them up."
Psalm 68:10

"He gives power to the weak, and to those who have no might, He increases strength. Even the youths shall faint and be weary, And the young men shall utterly fall, But those who wait on the LORD Shall renew their strength; They shall mount up with wings like eagles, They shall run and not be weary, They shall walk and not faint." Isaiah 40:29-31

When in doubt…
When hurting…
When the future seems unclear…
"Wait on the LORD: Be of good courage, and He shall strengthen your heart: Wait, I say, on the LORD." Psalm 27:14

It is folly to do something and expect nothing to happen. #33

Maybe you have seen or played with this clever toy.

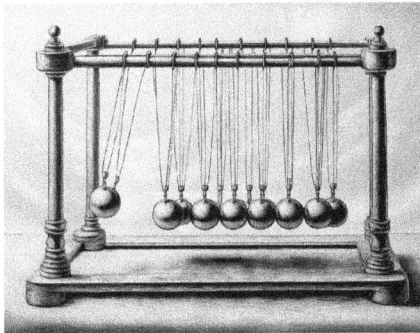

It is called Newton's Cradle, named after the brilliant scientist Sir Isaac Newton. He gave us the third law of motion, stating, "For every action, there is an equal and opposite reaction."

We can easily apply this concept to actions in our lives.

You may have heard of the "butterfly effect." The belief is that a butterfly will flap its wings on one side of the globe, and that insect's

tiny swoosh of air:
- moves a leaf
- which initiates a breeze
- that becomes a wind
- that pushes clouds and
- eventually causes a hurricane halfway around the world.

That theory, as fantastic as it sounds, contains much truth.

What you and I do today may ripple forward for decades to come. Good choices yield positive and uplifting outcomes. Poor choices bring about pain and agony and "knots" that are very hard to ever untangle, even to the point of affecting future generations.

Ecclesiastes 11:1-6 are the verses behind this concept. *"Sow seeds of goodness every day, even when it doesn't make sense to do so. At the right time, you will reap a reward. Be diligent about sowing goodness, and accept no excuses! Then goodness will become a part of who you are, not just a thing you do, and the world will be a better place because of it."*

I wish someone had told me sooner #34
about the importance of a wholesome Christian HUG.

"Greet one another with a holy kiss" is a phrase that appears in 2 Corinthians 13:12 and numerous other New Testament letters written by different Bible authors.

I went to Cuba with a team from my church to do construction work for a struggling congregation. Following their morning and evening Sunday services, the team members were all asked to line up in the front area of the church near the platform. Every female from the congregation, young and old, filed past us, and they all kissed each of us on one or both cheeks. It was their tradition, and how they affirmed and thanked us.

With that as background, let's look instead at the Americanized version of this practice—the double-arm "bear hug."

There has been extensive scientific research about the health benefits from hugs of affirmation. The results of these studies have shown that hugs help to reduce stress and pain. They also improve immune and cardiovascular health. This research found that these wholesome and affirming hugs lessen the odds of a person getting sick.

A "hug study" by scientists used two groups of people. The heart rates and blood pressure readings of the group members who gave and received hugs were measurably lower. However, in the group whose members sat side by side without hugging, there was no reduction in blood pressure or heart rate.

Hugs can make you happier.
Oxytocin levels rise when we hug, touch, or even sit close to someone else. Oxytocin is associated with happiness and less stress. Oxytocin causes a lowering of the stress hormone norepinephrine.

How many hugs do we need?
Family therapist Virginia Satir said, "We each need four hugs daily for survival. We need eight hugs a day for maintenance. And we need 12

hugs a day for personal growth."

That may sound like a lot of hugs, but research has proven that more hugs are better than fewer hugs.

So, if you've ever been on the fence about this topic, consider that renowned scientists AND Bible writers Paul, James, and Peter agree on the importance of the wholesome holy hug.

God's promises #35 are covenants with His people, and He is incapable of reneging on them (unlike you and me).

For several weeks in my Life Group on Sundays, our teacher has spoken for the entire hour about covenants. There is a term within that teaching that I had not heard of. The Bible refers to "cutting covenant." I learned that it was common in Old Testament times for two people to make a covenant by cutting an animal in half, separating the halves, and then walking between the pieces to seal the oath. While walking amid the split animal, each person swore they would meet the same end as the sacrificed animal if they broke their part of the agreement.

God has made incredible covenants with us, and the Bible expresses hundreds of them.

We make promises to each other and then break them with little regard for our integrity, assuming: *"They'll understand why I didn't show up..."* or *"It doesn't really matter that much. She'll get over it..."*

On the other hand, when God makes a covenant with us, He will...
- absolutely
- always
- every time
- without question
- for sure
- doubtless and
- certainly fulfill his covenant promises.

He would cease to be holy if He ever failed to keep just one of the promises He has made.

Here is a covenant promise that you can carry through this day, or close your eyes in peace and fall asleep tonight as you consider everything it means for you.

"The LORD Himself goes before you and will be with you; He will never leave you nor forsake you. Do not be afraid; do not be discouraged." Deuteronomy 31:8

Be careful when choosing #36 the source of your comfort.

There is a famous whiskey with the unlikely name of "Southern Comfort." My definition of comfort doesn't include the near certainty of a damaged liver, a D.U.I., and a marriage or family on the rocks.

Comfort can be deceiving. The serpent in the Garden of Eden promoted comfort by offering God-like wisdom through a bite of the fruit of a tree. The Sirens of Greek mythology beckoned sailors with their alluring voices to "Come hither!" The problem for the seamen, if they heeded the call, was the jagged rocks nearby that would surely tear their ships to bits.

Today, the devil still tempts millions with offers of short-term comfort through:
- Possessions
- Social status

- Sex outside of marriage
- Illicit substances and alcohol

The problem with these and other worldly distractions is that each one destroys lives, and all of them are temporary. They are not sustainable or productive.

- Money isn't limitless
- Health isn't guaranteed
- Time catches up with our bodies
- And sin always demands its payday

The Bible states in 2 Corinthians 1:3-4, *"God is the source of all comfort. He comforts us in all our troubles so that we can comfort others."*

The Latin roots of "comfort" are **con** and **forte**, meaning "to make strong together." According to the scriptures, comfort is more than just relaxation or having temporary relief from pain. Real comfort is the ability to rest in the knowledge that God is carrying our burdens and giving us the strength to keep going.

Whiskey can't do that. So, preach to yourself and warn others about where they should and shouldn't seek their comfort.

Needed: More pipes and conduits! #37

Along Israel's border with Jordan, you'll find the Dead Sea. It's known to be the lowest place on earth at 1,412 feet below sea level. Water from the land around it drains into this Sea, but no water flows out from it. It can't.

The city of New Orleans is a lot like a mini-Dead Sea. It was settled and populated as land below sea level. In a heavy storm or hurricane, excess rainwater must be pumped up and out, over the tops of seawall levees, and into the Mississippi River. If not, the city will fill up with water, just like a giant bowl.

When water only flows IN but cannot flow OUT, you have the makings of a cesspool—a sour and bitter and nasty and mosquito-infested area that is hard to enjoy. That's what happens in a bayou or a swamp.

This same thing occurs with your

life and mine. If we are hearing and seeing and taking in spiritual truths, but are not letting the uplifting INPUT flow OUTWARD from us, we are creating a "spiritual cesspool" of wasted truth that benefits no one but us.

The correct way, when God is blessing us through His favor and by the examples and biblical truths shared by others, is to be a free-flowing conduit—a pipeline—for those blessings. They come TO us, pass THROUGH us, and then move out through our words and acts TO others. We are expected to pass them along.

If we hold onto them, they will always rust and corrode, sour and decay.

The Israelites who hoarded the manna that God gave them for their meals saw this happen. In their 40 years in the wilderness, God always provided enough sweet-tasting manna for each day and a double serving for them to have for their Sabbath day. But when the manna appeared on the ground the other six mornings, if a person gathered extra planning to hold on to it, that manna was bitter and rancid when he ate it.

In Luke 12, Jesus is explaining this concept of hoarding our blessings:
"Then He told them a parable: 'The ground of a certain rich man produced an abundance. So he thought to himself,

'What shall I do, since I have nowhere to store my crops?' Then he said, 'This is what I will do: I will tear down my barns and will build bigger ones, and there I will store up all my grain and my goods. Then I will say to myself, "You have plenty of good things laid up for many years. Take it easy. Eat, drink, and be merry!" '
But God said to him, 'You fool! This very night, your life will be required of you. Then who will own what you have accumulated?"*

This is how it will be for anyone who stores up treasure for himself, but is not rich toward God and humanity out of His benefits.

God is taking you through various experiences day by day for your good and His greater purposes. Don't store them in warehouses as mere memories or even let them go to waste by *not* seeing their value. Continually ask God how you are to tell others of HIs goodness—the blessings that you have experienced. Even your story of the hard times that have come and gone will uplift someone's heart. Let your testimony bubble freely as cool, refreshing water flowing out of your life.

If Jesus isn't Lord OF all, He isn't Lord AT all. #38

Joshua had led the Israelites through deserts, rivers, and many trials for decades. If anyone on earth should have known God's faithfulness firsthand, it was those people. But they continued to waver in their commitment, unwilling to settle their loyalty once and for all. Do you remember how, within days after God visibly provided for their welfare, they denied God and made and worshipped a golden calf!?

Even the disciples, Jesus's trusted inner circle, ran and hid from the government leaders in Jerusalem on the night He was arrested. They knew Him, but in those hours, their fear overrode their affections. He wasn't first and foremost—their Lord. Their wishy-washy attitudes proved it.

"LORD" is defined as "the absolute master or ruler."

Most people don't truly surrender to the Lordship of Jesus. They say they commit, but each time those people fall away, they return to the altar steps and recommit themselves to God. This pattern typically happens again and again.

How many things do you and I commit ourselves to, but when our schedules get tight, or it's no longer convenient, we casually UNcommit?

No! We must SURRENDER to Jesus as Lord, Ruler, and Master. True surrender is once and forever!

The image that describes this best is when police officers surround the lawbreaker, and he is told to, "Come out with your hands in the air!" That is what surrendering to Jesus as Lord looks like. Hands above your head with no turning back! Once captured, we can't UNsurrender.

Any lesser response is mere pretense. Until we've fully surrendered, Jesus isn't our Lord.

It is God's will that you should be sanctified. #39 (1 Thessalonians 4:3)

This is an important topic, so please read this with care. Sanctification is a term you have undoubtedly heard, but, like me, you may not be able to define it easily.

That scripture in 1 Thessalonians chapter 4 continues with these other instructions:

"...that you should avoid sexual immorality; that each of you should learn to control your own body in a way that is holy and honorable, not in passionate lust like the pagans, who do not know God; and that in this matter no one should wrong or take advantage of a brother or sister. The Lord will punish all those who commit such sins."

You and I being sanctified is about far more than sexual purity alone. It is about being separated (set apart) for God's ultimate purposes for us.

In the Old Testament, we read that certain cups and utensils were "sanctified" — kept separate — for use in the Temple ceremonies.

But rather than mere objects, Leviticus 20:7-8 refers to people. *"Consecrate (separate) yourselves, therefore, and be holy; for I am the LORD your God. Keep my statutes, and do them; I am the LORD who sanctifies you."*

Precisely, what does that look like in your life or mine? Sanctification is a lifelong process initiated and continued by God to make a believer increasingly like Jesus. With that occurring, GOD has a role, and WE each have a role.

God lays out the "track" for us, and we ride on His "train."

The "train" for us involves reading, studying, meditating on biblical truth privately, and being taught in a corporate setting (in church) from the word of God. It includes praying, fellowshiping, giving, and sharing the gospel. Simply put, the process of sanctification is evident in an obedient life, which continually moves toward a deeper Christian experience. The process won't be complete (the train will never arrive) until we reach Heaven. But we press forward with intentionality!

So, to come back to the original command, we are sanctified by faithfully doing the things that are the best for our growth anyway, and it's those things that will always bring us the most satisfaction!

It will happen most often after you have finished college and # 40

entered the workforce. It generally occurs when someone says, "Tell me about yourself."
Most people respond with:
- "I work at…"

or

- "I'm a… sales rep for…"
- "an engineer/employee at…"
- "an attorney with…" Etc.

We wrongly get our identity from our job, from our ZIP Code, perhaps from our parents or family, our spouse's family, our children's accomplishments, or even the kind of vehicle we drive.

This is the 40th of the foundational elements, and it is:

Who I am isn't what I do or any of those other external things. It's who God created me to be and tells me I am.

Proof:

"No longer do I call you servants, for the servant does not know what his master is doing; but I have called you friends..." (John 15:15)

"See what kind of love the Father has given to us, that we should be called children of God..." (1 John 3:1)

"You shall be a crown of beauty in the hand of the Lord, and a royal diadem in the hand of your God..." (Isaiah 62:3)

"You are no longer a slave, but a son, and if a son, then an heir through God." (Galatians 4:7)

So you can rejoice! *"For in Christ Jesus you are all sons of God, through faith."* (Galatians 3:26)

I have one simple task to fulfill in my Christian life.

#41

In the workforce environment, every position has a written job description that lays out the employer's expectations. Our job as followers of Christ has been explained to us in thirteen words.

A catechism is a summary of a religious doctrine. In 1647, theologians in Great Britain came together to compile a lengthy and highly detailed statement of the Christian faith, known as the Westminster Larger Catechism..

The Westminster Shorter Catechism is familiar to many of us who have been in church for some time. In thirteen words, it simply says: "The chief duty of man is to glorify God and enjoy Him forever." That, my dear friend, is our job description.

So, how do I glorify God?

1. Praise Him with your lips.
2. Obey His Word.
3. Pray in Jesus' name.
4. Produce spiritual fruit.
5. Remain sexually pure.
6. Seek the good of others.
7. Give generously.
8. Live honorably among unbelievers.
9. Be faithful when persecuted.
10. Face death with faith.

To enjoy Him forever, simply remain under the "faucet" from which His blessings flow and receive them freely and gladly.

We praise God, NOT for #42 what He does, but because of who He is.

Proof: Psalm 145:3 says, *"Great is the LORD and most worthy of praise; His greatness no one can fathom."*

  * We are commanded to praise: Psalm 150:6 says, *"Let everything that has breath praise the Lord."*
  * Praise invites God's presence, allowing us to experience His benefits: Psalm 22:3 says, *"God inhabits the praises of His people."*
  * Praise is how we approach God for an audience with Him: Psalm 100:4 says, *"Enter His gates with thanksgiving and His courts with praise."*
  * Praise is our path out of despair: Isaiah 61:3 says it is *"...the oil of gladness instead of mourning."*
  * Praise is how our spirits are raised: David says, *"In His presence,*

there is fullness of joy!"
* Praise is the best way to express thanks to God: Psalm 107:21-22 says, *"Let them give thanks to the Lord for his unfailing love and his wonderful deeds for mankind."*
* Praise opens the door to miracles: Acts 16:25-26 describes how Paul and Silas were praying and singing hymns to God in prison, and the prison doors flew open.

Let me assure you that there will be seasons when you have no desire to offer any praise. Your glass will be empty, and your strength will seem small. It is on those days and at those moments that you will have to take authority over your downtrodden self and tell your mind and body to praise God. Lift your head, straighten your shoulders, raise your hands, and say, *"Heart, I command you to praise God!"* Be expectant and refreshed by what happens next!

I need to wash someone's feet.

#43

At every stage of Jesus's three-year ministry with the 12 disciples, He knew their thoughts. He knew their wavering commitments to his mission on earth and to Him.

Jesus saw their lack of understanding when the crowds came to listen or to be healed. He saw how the disciples wanted to send the 5,000 men (probably 15,000 people) away hungry rather than feed them. Jesus saw their faithlessness that night while He was on the boat with them, and the storm arose on the sea.

But He cared greatly for them anyway.

In the upper room, with the full scope of events on His mind that would happen the following day—and how He would soon die—guess what Jesus did. He removed His outer garment, took a basin of water, tied a towel around His waist, and, one by one, washed the nasty, calloused feet of the flawed and wavering men around Him—those men He dearly loved anyway.

The image of that scene is almost incomprehensible. No one before had served others so selflessly! Jesus, the Creator of everything, is kneeling. He finishes washing and drying one person's feet, slides the water basin over, and scoots Himself to the next and then the next. He probably spent most of an hour serving His friends in the most humbling posture that any man can assume.

You and I have the privilege of yielding ourselves daily to this amazing Jesus. He knows how weak and wishy-washy I am, and you are, but He willingly *"...humbled himself and became obedient unto death, even the death of the cross..."* (Philippians 2:8). He did this for us to rescue us from eternal separation from Himself and give us the best possible futures. All He asks is for us to come to our senses, turn away from our sins in repentance, and commit our forevers to Him. As a response and as a free gift, He exchanges our filthy "clothes" and gives us His righteousness in return.

Just as Jesus asked His disciples in the garden before his betrayal, *"Can you not stay true to me for only an hour?"* He still asks us to draw from His unending reservoir of power and live for Him.

Some people consider it archaic, backwoods, and fringe. But Jesus's example for us is timeless and crystal clear. Somebody in your world longs to experience the touch of unconditional acceptance through your humble service. It is a statement of deep commitment and radical loving care as you *literally*, or *at the very least*, *figuratively*, wash a friend's feet.

W.W.J.D. (What Would Jesus Do?)
There you have it in black and white!

In a previous devotional, we said, *"It is folly to do something and expect nothing to happen."* The key takeaway from that is there are ripples that spread out from all our actions—good or bad—and they continually impact the world around us.

#44

Equally important is the foolishness of doing NOTHING but expecting SOMETHING to happen.

People all around us are standing on the sidelines of life, waiting for a parade that they can step in front of and claim as their own, co-opting someone else's labors. They are **waiters** and **delayers** rather than **doers**.

God calls us all to be initiators, creators, and workers. He began that calling in the first pages of the Bible.

Proof:
Genesis 2:15
"The Lord God took the man and put him in the Garden of Eden to work it and care for it."

Proof:
Proverbs 12:11
"Those who work their land will have abundant food, but those who chase fantasies have no sense."

Proof:
Colossians 3:23
"Whatever you do, work at it with all your heart, as working for the Lord, not for human masters."

And A Warning!:
"For even when we were with you, we gave you this rule: 'The one who is unwilling to work shall not eat.'" (2 Thessalonians 3:10)

So with clean hands and a pure heart, DO SOMETHING today that will matter for eternity!

God loves your BIG and BOLD prayers.

#45

The Bible tells us of only two people in the three years of Jesus's public ministry who caused the Savior to marvel—the Roman Centurion and the Canaanite woman. They both displayed great faith—the first by asking Jesus to heal his servant. The second person was an unimpressive woman who boldly asked Jesus to heal her sick daughter.

You may recall from Matthew 8 that when Jesus arrived in Capernaum, a centurion came to Jesus, asking for his help because the man's servant was paralyzed and in great pain. Jesus offered to accompany the centurion to where the servant was. But the soldier said that wouldn't be necessary—that Jesus could speak a healing word from afar, and it would be sufficient.

Jesus marveled at the centurion's faith.

Then, in Matthew 15, we learn of the Canaanite woman who petitioned the Lord, asking that Jesus heal her daughter who was sick. Jesus's initial response might have seemed to lack compassion, but in reality, he was testing the woman's mettle—her determination. When she persisted, can't you picture the smile crossing Jesus's lips and the delight in his eyes? So, of course—absolutely—Jesus granted her request!

There is no limit to the riches of our Lord. His boundless supply is sufficient for your and my every need! Nothing asked in accordance with His will is refused!

The bigger the need, the greater the glory that God receives. You are invited to drink from the fountain, which will never run dry!

Proof:
Jesus is speaking.
"I say to you, if you have faith as a mustard seed, you will say to this mountain, 'Move from here to there,' and it will move, and nothing will be impossible for you." Matthew 17:20

Proof:
While battling the Amalekites, Joshua, a man

like us, asked God in faith to stop the earth from turning for a full day so the sun could continue to light the sky, giving his soldiers time to defeat Israel's enemy. (from Joshua 10)

Proof:
"Don't be troubled about anything, but in everything, by prayer and supplication with thanksgiving, let your requests be made known unto God. And the peace of God, which passeth all understanding, will keep your hearts and minds settled by Christ Jesus."
Philippians 4:6,7

If a tiny speck of faith offered by a Roman soldier, the plea of a simple woman, and the petition of an ordinary man can result in a healing, holding the sun in place, and moving a mountain, imagine what *your* big and bold faith placed in the Creator of everything can accomplish!

If I am comfortable with my sin, I have not encountered the living God. #46

The apostle John, when he was allowed a glimpse into Heaven, as told in Revelation, should be our example. His awe of the Son of God caused him to fall to his knees as if he were undone.

Have you ever been around someone who had such a close walk with God that you felt, in comparison, your weaknesses and sins were exposed and glaring—that your face and posture would reveal what you hoped to hide?

I had that experience when I attended a retreat led by Bertha Smith, an 80-something-year-old former missionary to China. I arrived with a few dozen others, expecting to learn about deeper prayer. However, my frailties and compromises, which I had not yet repented of, made me so uncomfortable in the presence of this saintly woman that I didn't want her eyes to meet mine. I imagined and feared that she would read my thoughts.

John tells us in Revelation chapter one that while in Heaven, admiring its awesomeness, he heard a voice speaking to him. When he turned to the "figure of a man," he saw:
- Jesus's face was like "the sun shining with full force"
- The sword from his mouth represented his judgment
- His feet were like burnished bronze, conveying stability and strength
- And Jesus had eyes like fire that pierced into John's innermost self

You see, absolutely nothing will be hidden from the Lord Jesus on the day when you and I, like John, will stand before the Creator of everything.

Bertha Smith, that petite and dear saint, didn't know me, but her humble countenance intimidated me. Jesus, however, knows *everything* I've ever done and every thought I've ever had. He sees my heart and intentions.

I must become so *UNcomfortable* with my sin that I allow Jesus to cleanse me—here, now, and daily—to be as white as snow.

And so should you.

God can't steer a parked car. #47

This concept came to my attention through my pastor, Dr. Alan Floyd.

We have discussed the importance of God NOT being your co-pilot. He needs to be at the controls, single-handedly flying the "airplane" of your life. Your place and mine are in the back seat or, better yet, in the cargo compartment. God doesn't need our counsel or advice on which route to take.

As crucial as that truism is, when it comes to guiding you through day-to-day challenges and decisions, you and I would do well to cooperate with God. He will not attach a tow rope to your life and pull you around town. You and I would be bruised and bloodied if we continually resisted His tugs and guidance.

You can KNOW what God is doing and where He is leading you. It requires listening and focus. Just like the air around you is full of broadcast signals, only a radio tuned to an active frequency will receive the information or the music.

God is always moving and speaking (transmitting) to His children, but you and I must be attentive to His voice and practice listening to Him.

Proof;
"And your ears shall hear a word behind you, saying, 'This is the way, walk in it,' when you turn to the right or when you turn to the left." (Isaiah 30:21)

Sometimes we become paralyzed by uncertainty, fearing that we'll miss or fail to recognize God's perfect will for us. Being cautious is a mature response. Being frozen by fear is NOT normal or healthy.

A wise person who wants to make informed decisions as they seek to know God's mind will consider one, many, or ALL of these points. First and foremost,
- PRAY! You can do many things after you pray, but nothing is more important than praying UNTIL you pray. Your prayers are never intended to influence God. Instead, they are to move you and transform your heart so that it aligns with God's perfect plan.
- SEARCH the scriptures! The total revealed wisdom of God is contained in the Word of God. The 66 Old and New Testament books offer principles that will always transfer directly to your 21st-century questions. As

you search, don't close your eyes and drop your finger on a random page, expecting to find the answer you need. Instead, read regularly, study, and meditate on scripture. You'll be amazed at how God will enlighten specific passages to meet your essential needs and answer your sincere questions exactly when necessary.

• SEEK wise counsel - Ask the opinions of people in your life who demonstrate stable, God-honoring lifestyles. As long as their advice aligns with the Bible, consider their opinions. And ask them to pray for you.

Let the peace of God be your guide as you consider His prompting! Until you receive your answer, keep your "car" in "Drive" and continue moving forward, simply doing what you have been doing until now. Be patient. God has never been late!

I need to sign my contract with God before He fills in the blanks.

#48

Surrendering to God's plan means that I put aside MY plans in favor of HIS before I ever know what His will for my future might be.

A friend of mine was worried after he gave his heart to Jesus as Savior. He feared that God would tell him to go and be a missionary in the darkest part of the African Congo.

That isn't the character of God at all! God isn't going to save a football linebacker and then turn him into a ballet dancer. God's nature is to take your strengths—the strengths He has given you—and launch you on a path to becoming the best YOU possible.

God is the perfect Father, especially to those of us (everyone!) who had a good but imperfect one here on earth. His desire for us is always to experience the best. After all, He sent Jesus to purchase our redemption. How could we not trust Him to unfold plans that far exceed our own?

Proof:
"Therefore, I urge you, brothers and sisters, because of God's mercy, to offer your bodies as a living sacrifice, holy and pleasing to God—this is your true and proper worship." (Romans 12:1)

"Trust in the Lord with all your heart and lean not on your understanding; in all your ways submit to him, and he will make your paths straight." (Proverbs 3:5,6)

"For I know the plans I have for you," declares the Lord, *"plans to prosper you and not to harm you, plans to give you hope and a future."* (Jeremiah 29:11)

If you can trust God with your eternity, you can certainly trust Him with your Tuesdays, Fridays, and tomorrows.

I am greatly loved #49

and highly favored by God, but I don't get a "pass" when I knowingly compromise with sin.

There are no teacher's pets among us. God's standard to which everyone must rise is perfection. However, we cannot achieve this in our strength or by our own will. That's why people need the Lord and other Christians.

Jesus knows our tendencies to wander and weave and cross the centerline—to leave the lane of holiness. This is why guardrails exist on life's roads.

Still, the loving Good Shepherd carries his staff with the crook at the end. You've seen those drawings and images. It's shaped like that so He can reach into the thorns and bushes and pull us back to Himself.

Proof:

"But you, O Lord, are a God merciful and gracious, slow to anger and abounding in steadfast love and faithfulness." (Psalm 86:15)

"The Lord is slow to anger and rich in steadfast love, forgiving iniquity and transgression, but he will by no means overlook the guilty..." (Numbers 14:18)

Notice the last words of the verse. God doesn't grade on the curve. God's patience is not limitless. He won't wink at our sin. He will always maintain His standards. Thankfully, every tool and benefit (the Bible, a thriving church with great preaching, the fellowship of other brothers) that we need to rise to God's expectations is available. We simply need to make use of them.

The Bible can keep you from sin, and sin will keep you from the Bible.

#50

My dad wrote that statement on the opening page of a Bible he gave me for my 13th birthday. I later learned that those words weren't original to him, but they came from a sermon preached 150 years earlier by D.L. Moody.

Dwight L. Moody was born in 1837. He quit school after the 5th grade and left home at 17 to begin a job selling shoes. Unsuccessful and not following the Lord in Boston, at the age of 18, Moody gave his life to Jesus. Soon after that, with no training whatsoever, he began preaching and ministering to soldiers on the battlefields during the American Civil War.

Amazingly, in just a few years, the barely literate Moody started a seminary and two colleges. In Chicago in 1886,

Moody Bible College was founded. It is stronger than ever today, and almost 50,000 students have graduated from there.

It is estimated that in his lifetime, including in the U.S. and numerous countries worldwide, Dwight L. Moody, untrained but willing, preached face-to-face to 100 million people.

Circling back to the words at the beginning of this devotional, understand from Moody's example that a focused life, knowing and following the truths of the Bible, is capable of doing anything God can do.

Has the Bible kept you from sin, or has your sin kept you away from reading and loving the Bible?

A little effort becomes much when it is placed in the Master's hands. Imagine what God could do with your surrendered abilities, demonstrating to others the power of the gospel.

Let God prove Himself strong for His purposes and glory through YOUR life!

God can't use you publicly until He teaches you privately.

#51

I first heard that statement while sitting under the teaching of a brilliant layman in Mobile, Alabama.

After John the Apostle baptized Jesus, the Lord left to be alone in the wilderness to fast and pray. In that desolate place with no one around to encourage him, he was tempted by Satan.

Three times, Satan approached Jesus with legitimate offers. The first was of bread to ease his hunger. The second attempt was to have Jesus flaunt His divinity by throwing Himself from a high place so that angels would save Him. The final effort by Satan was to have Jesus worship him and receive all the kingdoms of the world.

In every instance, Jesus responded and rebuffed the devil with scripture. Jesus knew the Word of God, and He withstood His and our enemy. Because of this, he passed every test with a perfect score!

From that wilderness classroom, after 40 days, God led Jesus back into the day-to-day world to begin His public ministry.

How long has it been since you've gotten away from the traffic of life, the noises of social media, and the mind buzz of your plans?

Do you know how to resist the offers of Satan? Do you want to be used by God to make a difference in your circle—your place in the world? If so, you and I need to make time each day to enter our private place and stay there until God has taught us an important truth or two. Only then will we be useful for greater things.

God can't and won't use you or me publicly until He tutors us privately.

W e've reached the 52nd foundational truth. #**52**

Disney World doesn't sell bubble gum.

For that matter, they don't sell any other kind of gum. You might have already known this. I only learned about it a few years ago. By being proactive, they don't have a problem with sticky gunk on their sidewalks or pink clumps sticking to their guests' shoes. They deal with the issue before it becomes a problem. They nip it in the bud!

That approach is a version of how you and I should manage conflicts and misunderstandings.

If we allow ourselves to be easily offended, we have purposefully stepped on a proverbial wad of bubble gum. We'll fixate on the sticky lump underfoot until we scrape it and rid ourselves of the stringy mess.

The Bible calls this response (holding tightly onto our hurts) a "root of bitterness." However, if we brush off the petty criticisms or unfair rejections, the root of bitterness has no soil in which to grow.

In 1 Corinthians 13, widely called "The Love Chapter," we read this: *"Love does not demand its way. It is not irritable or touchy. It does not hold grudges AND WILL HARDLY EVEN NOTICE WHEN OTHERS DO THEM WRONG."* Do you see the emphasis? That is how you and I stay cheerful among spiteful people. Just strap on your blinders, secure them tightly, and press on ahead!

Statistics show that most people within the reach and range of the stone you might throw don't have a relationship with Jesus. They often lack the ability to be kind, compassionate, or even truthful. They chew gum and then drop it on YOUR sidewalk.

Your response today and every day should be to put on Teflon-soled sneakers and then step carefully amongst their juicy and thoughtless landmines! Avoid them. That's how you deal with their problems lest they become your problems.

H ow does a pane of glass become strong enough to serve as a door, a tabletop, or even a wall? It occurs when a regular piece of glass—the kind you would find in a photo frame—is placed into intense heat. It's baked at a temperature of 1,000 degrees and then rapidly cooled under high pressure. The result is tempered glass that can be almost as strong as steel.

#53

Extreme heat and then frigid cold, occurring under high pressure, are the causes of this phenomenon. HEAT and then COLD with PRESSURE—those things don't weaken the glass. They enhance and improve it for the rigors of hard abuse.

Here is the 53rd of the foundational principles that you should know.

You can't have a testimony without a test.

My great friend Ben related those words to me during his treatment for a rare skull tumor. His was a test that cost him most of his 18th year—half of his senior year of high school and several months thereafter.

I have given a lot of thought to the tests I have undergone. None of mine were ones I sought or welcomed, and none have been nearly as intense or as lengthy as Ben's.

Your tests will expose your weaknesses, but they can declare your strengths. James 1:3 says that the testing of our faith will bring about patience.

There is a parallel in this glass illustration to the trials of life. The "heat" of difficult circumstances certainly will come, maybe even today. When others around you wither and falter, what will be the results of your test?

For the prepared man or woman, when unkind people and unexpected circumstances assail you, if you have your spiritual roots anchored deep into good "soil," you will survive, thrive, and have a testimony after the test to tell of God's goodness.

I coined a phrase a few **# 54** months ago—at least, I *think* it was my doing. I don't recall hearing it from anyone else.

Here is #54 of the principles that can strengthen your faith walk.

The first look is free, but the second look sets the hook.

A man's attention is captured through his eyes. A touch is what normally attracts a woman.

You and I cannot always keep from seeing something that is tempting or alluring. That first look is often unavoidable, and it, at that point, is not a sin. However, when we FAIL to turn away and we LINGER there, the "hook" gets implanted. From there, we begin to formulate a plan to desire, possess, or respond with our flesh to what we've seen.

By not averting our eyes and turning away, the likelihood of us carrying out the sin that the devil and his forces are dangling before us—those odds rise quickly and exponentially!

Therefore, the best plan is to avoid altogether the places and circumstances that have led to our past downfalls. You know exactly where your weaknesses and blind spots are. You know where you've been or what you were doing when you have failed in the past. Common sense says you should never, ever return to that setting.

Proverbs contains wisdom and warnings about "being wise..." and "being watchful..." From the book of James, we see our role in staying pure. We initiate, and God responds. James 4:7-8 says, "*Resist the devil, and he will flee from you. Come near to God* (your part), *and He will come near you.*" (God's response).

Ceasing old habits is essential, but we must fill the voids with new and positive actions.

No one suddenly commits grievous sins. Those failures occur when we compromise in a series of small ways. Soon enough, we are facing a major crisis—one where Satan always has the upper hand. It's the "frog in the boiling water story" all over again. The frog gets into the cool water and relaxes. Someone turns on the stove burner, and the water slowly warms. The frog acclimates to the conditions over time until, eventually, the simmering water becomes boiling water. By then, it's too late. The frog is cooked.

The single most important component in success over sexual sin is saturating your mind with truth. That truth will come from reading and meditating on scripture. Pursuing conversations with others who are mature in their faith walks is helpful. Intentionally seeking to be filled with the Holy Spirit (a faith request in prayer) is absolutely vital.

The chances of failure in an unguarded moment are significantly reduced IF you regularly fill your spirit life with truth, uplifting music, good counsel, and scriptural teachings. Your strength to resist will come from these things. And don't hesitate to wear your Bible out!!

You have heard the adage that a recovering alcoholic has no business walking on the sidewalk that takes him past the liquor store. He is wise to intentionally cross the street to the other sidewalk. So should we with our thoughts.

Avoid the hook. Don't continue to look.

Proof:
Psalm 37:27-29: *"Flee from evil and do good, and dwell forever."*
• 2 Timothy 2:22-24: *"Run from the evil desires of youth, and pursue righteousness, faith, love, and peace."*
• Proverbs 4:14-19: *"Don't take the path of the wicked; don't follow those who do evil."*

My heart is a liar. Yours is, too. #55

Well-meaning friends often share sweet-sounding counsel when they urge you to "…Just follow your heart…" That advice is incredibly harmful once you understand what the Bible says about us in our natural state.

Jeremiah 17:9 tells us, *"The heart is the worst sort of deceiver, and the wickedness that comes from it knows no limits. No one can truly explain it."*

The term "heart" is a metaphor for the core of a person's identity. This includes our thoughts, emotions, and our will. Jeremiah's use of the term "heart" reminds us that relying on our feelings—our "gut"— will often lead us to dangerous places.

Understanding this truth, you and I should regularly pray for a renewed mind that is aligned with God's wisdom.

At every fork in the road, we face two choices. One option is the broad way—a smooth path lined with gorgeous scenery. The other one offers rugged, even barren terrain. The Bible speaks of this very scenario in Matthew 17, and it is worth noting that things aren't always as they appear on the surface. It reports, *"Wide is the gate, and broad is the path that will lead to your destruction. Most people go that way. But the other road is narrow, and the gate is small, and it leads to life. Only a few choose this path."*

So, when making the little and indeed the life-changing decisions, seek to know God's mind. Don't rely on the impulses and the feelings of your heart.

When you were born, you begin to die. Plan accordingly.

#56

A close friend of mine, a couple of years out of college, was working on a house framing crew in the sweltering July temperatures of Iowa. From high on the attic rafters of an unfinished house, he blacked out and collapsed 30 feet to the concrete below. He never attempted to break his fall. With no brain activity, doctors removed life support the following day.

Brian and I had spoken at 7:00 on the morning before he fell. It was his last day on the job before moving home to California. He had packed his car for the trip. A few days earlier, I had sent him a set of sermon CDs for his 24 hours of solo westward driving time with his dog alongside him.

My friend's dad had died unexpectedly a few weeks earlier, and Brian was moving home to comfort and encourage his mom and sister as they all processed their family's loss.

After Brian's death, I pulled a book from my shelf—one I had begun but not gotten far into. Its title was *Heaven*, written by a retired pastor named Randy Alcorn. Suddenly, the book became very important to me, and I read every word eagerly, learning what the Bible says about Heaven. Beyond many verses describing Heaven, some of the author's words were speculative but based on logical guesses.

One statement he made has stayed with me. It concerns the unanswerable "Why?" concerning death. Alcorn stated, **We have to get to Heaven somehow.**

For those who have a relationship with Christ,
    * Death is just a doorway.
    * Heaven is the destination.
    * Hearing "Well done!" is our goal.

A faulty foundation = a foolhardy life. # #57

When planning new high-rise buildings in countries along the Pacific Rim or in other earthquake-prone areas, their foundations can extend very deep—well over 200 feet underground.

Even nature demonstrates this. California's giant redwood trees, many of which have stood tall and strong for centuries, have root systems that interlock with those of other nearby redwoods. That provides them and others with added stability and strength when strong winds blow or the earth shakes.

In Matthew 7, Jesus instructs us on the foundation that is essential for a stable, fulfilled, and purposeful life.

> *"Everyone who hears my words and does them will be like a wise man who built his house on the rock. The*

rain fell, the floods came, and the winds blew and beat on that house, but it stood strong because it had been founded and built on the rock. All others who hear these words of mine but do not do them will be like a foolish man who built his house on the sand. For them, the rain fell, and the floods came, and the winds blew and beat against that house, and it fell, and great was the fall of it."

Anchors are a big deal when rough seas are threatening. The first hurricane I experienced was Frederic in 1979. I was new to the coastal area of Alabama, and I was aware of a wealthy family in the county who owned a 105-foot-long luxury yacht. There was no dock or boat slip large enough or sturdy enough to protect that ship from the predicted winds and waves, so they anchored it in the middle of Mobile Bay. Twenty-four hours later, following 130 mph sustained winds with 20-foot seas—after the storm passed—the ship had survived.

The practical application of this should constantly direct our thinking—to next week, next year, and beyond. Ask yourself:
• How prepared am I for the storms of my

tomorrows?

• How does my anticipation of eternity factor into what I am doing today?

• Am I linking my life with others around me for difficult days that will surely come?

• Is my foundation rooted deeply and anchored to Jesus?"

My future hope isn't limited by my present situation or abilities. #58

Think with me about one of the characteristics of God. He is sovereign. The sovereignty of God, as it relates to Christianity, can be defined as God's right to exercise His ruling power over His creation.

- No one is higher than Him.
- No one is wiser.
- No one is more aware.
- No one is more just.
- No one is more faithful and dependable.
- No one is more merciful.

Jesus is your advocate to the Father, continually expressing His thoughts about you. He prays that your and my doubts will become faith.

Are your hands pure, empty, and

open to receive His goodness? Then God gives me much hope for you. You are aligned with His requirements for the full range of blessings.

The Greek word for hope isn't the same as our everyday use of the term. We "hope" it doesn't rain so we can have a picnic. We "hope" our team wins. No, the hope mentioned in the Bible gives zero place for the possibility that it WON'T come to pass.

In the scriptures, hope is the confident expectation of future good, especially concerning God's faithfulness and promises. Hope doesn't fade or waver even in the face of the most challenging circumstances. Hope expresses not wishful thinking but a strong and solid trust in the character of God and His plans to uphold and rescue you.

So, remember
- Who loves you
- Who died for you
- Who redeemed you
- Who prays for you
- Who provides each heartbeat and breath for you
- Who has a plan for you!

If, as best you know how, you have transferred your trust and hope from your inabilities to God's capabilities, you are in the cleft of the rock and under His wings. And you'll be just fine!

Romans 15:13 ~ *"May the God of hope fill you with all joy and peace in believing, so that by the power of the Holy Spirit, you may abound in hope."*

Matthew 10:29 - *"Isn't the price of two sparrows a penny? Even so, if either of them falls to the ground, they are never outside the Father's care."*

The 59th foundational principle tells me that **# 59**

I can live free of fear, regardless of my circumstances.

Beginning on December 16, 1811, a little bit north of Memphis, the small town of New Madrid, Missouri, was hit by a series of strong earthquakes. They caused widespread damage across thousands of square miles over several days. The intensity was so great that, for a while, the nearby Mississippi River flowed BACKWARDS. Those quakes shook so violently that they caused church bells to ring in New York City and Boston, more than a thousand miles away.

I've never been in an earthquake. I have several friends who grew up in California, and they've tried to describe to me what it feels like to have the floor shift beneath you, for books to fall from shelves, and for hanging lamps to swing freely overhead. They say if you are outdoors, the ground around you can roll like waves under your feet. That would terrify me. We expect our cities, neighborhoods, and homes to be stable, but even in South Alabama, there have been instances of shifting underground plates.

Every morning is packed with new mercies for you and me. Here's a sure word you can cling to today. It can steady your legs when the future feels uncertain.

Isaiah 54:10
"The mountains might vanish, and the hills might shudder, but My love and kindness will not be taken from you. My pledge of peace will not be shaken," says the Lord, who extends His loving care over you.

Psalm 46:2 - *"We won't fear when earthquakes come and the mountains break apart and tumble into the sea."*

We can have total assurance that God will hold us firmly, no matter what happens around us and to us. Tell your heart to believe this truth!

As we reach the final **#60** block of our foundation, remember this truth:

It is far better to look ahead with hope than to dwell on the past with longing or regret.

Jesus said, *"No one who puts a hand to the plow and looks back is fit for service in the kingdom of God."* (Luke 9:62)

Consider Lot and his wife, as mentioned in Genesis 19 and Luke 17. Two angels had visited Lot, telling him to take his family and flee Sodom and Gomorrah, because God was going to destroy those cities due to their great sins. Lot and his family were told NOT to look back as they left. However, for reasons of her own, Lot's wife disobeyed. We know about her fate from that action.

Many scholars believe she left those cities begrudgingly, taking with her memories of the rowdy times and decadence that flowed freely in that infamous place.

You and I cannot plow or plant a straight furrow if our attention is given to the ground that's behind us.

The apostle Paul boldly stated in Philippians 3: *"...One thing I do: Forgetting what is behind and straining toward what is ahead, I press on toward the goal to win the prize for which God has called me heavenward in Christ Jesus."*

Your windshield is 100 times larger than your rearview mirror. Face forward. Leave your failures and frustrations at the foot of the cross. Focus on what's ahead of you, not what's behind you. For the follower of Christ, there is absolutely nothing in your past life that you still need!

This page is intentionally blank

Epilogue

A final challenge...

I earned my pilot's license in 1976 while I was on the staff of the Contemporary Christian music group "TRUTH."

Late one night I departed the tiny airport in Troy, Alabama and was headed for big Tampa International Airport. I was flying a Piper six-seater plane and my passengers were the leader of TRUTH, his wife, and the three female singers from the group.

There is an oddity in aviation that most people don't know of. It's a big deal, and paying attention to it can mean the difference between arriving at your destination or being many miles off course. It concerns the instrument panel's magnetic compass and a regular adjustment that is needed.

To maintain the desired course, a pilot in those days referred to his paper map (called a sectional) and also make a compass correction or two during a flight. The amount to correct depended on where you were at the moment and where you were heading.

In the southeast United States, the most significant compass error runs along an invisible line essentially from Miami to Detroit. It passes very close to the Alabama/Georgia border.

If you depended on your magnetic compass and flew anywhere near that invisible line, but you didn't bother to correct for up to 5 degrees of course error, you would THINK you were headed in the right direction, but you could end up far away from where you had planned.

That night, I made the compass correction at the correct time and location during my flight, and we touched down in Tampa exactly as planned with no problems. Had I failed to follow that procedure, we might have ended up IN the Gulf waters.

Take this principle and apply it to our lives here on earth. If you drew a line forward from where you are today (the direction you are traveling spiritually, vocationally, in relationships, etc.), and you followed this path 2, 4, or 10 years into the future, where would that trajectory take you? Would you touchdown where you hoped to find yourself? Or somewhere else entirely?

The summer I turned 20, I took a long look at the direction my life was heading and the things that owned my heart. I got honest with myself, and I made a significant change of direction—a course correction.

I don't know anyone with worthwhile goals who hasn't stopped now and then to evaluate his career, relationships, use of time, and most of all, his relationship with God—then make a subtle or perhaps a dramatic course correction. It shows real wisdom to seek fresh and regular input and guidance from caring friends on life's road.

Socrates said it best: "An unexamined life is not worth living." I would add that a person who fails to honestly consider his goals, and observe correct waypoints to reach that destination in the light of God's will for him, is heading for disappointments—or even disaster.

Finally, the apostle Paul wrote: "*One thing I do: forgetting what lies behind and straining forward to what lies ahead, I press on toward the GOAL for the prize of the upward call of God in Christ Jesus.*" Philippians 3:13,14

www.ingramcontent.com/pod-product-compliance
Lightning Source LLC
Chambersburg PA
CBHW020949030426
42339CB00004B/12